Harry Okpik, Determined Musher

Nunavummi

The Nunavummi reading series is a Nunavut-developed levelled book series that supports literacy development while teaching readers about the people, traditions, and environment of the Canadian Arctic.

Published in Canada by Nunavummi, an imprint of
Inhabit Education Books Inc. | www.inhabiteducation.com

Inhabit Education Books Inc.
(Iqaluit) P.O. Box 2129, Iqaluit, Nunavut, X0A 1H0
(Toronto) 191 Eglinton Avenue East, Suite 301, Toronto, Ontario, M4P 1K1

Printed in Canada.

ISBN: 978-1-77450-201-3

INHABIT
EDUCATION
BOOKS

Harry Okpik, Determined Musher

WRITTEN BY

Maren Vsetula & Harry Okpik

ILLUSTRATED BY

Ali Hinch

Who Is Harry Okpik?

Harry is an Inuk man from Nunavik, which is in northern Quebec. He knows what it means to work hard. He has a dog team, a family, and a full-time job. He works as an Uumajut Warden, which is a type of wildlife officer.

Harry has had many adventures, as well as a number of challenges. Harry's adventures started when he was a boy living on the land. He always wanted to be a musher with his own dog team, but he had a difficult path to get there. This is the story of Harry Okpik and some of his adventures.

Churchill

Hudson Bay

Quaqtaq

Ungava
Bay

Montreal

3

Early Memories

Harry was born in the small town of Quaqtaq. People lived in camps on the land at that time. Harry grew up in tents and *igluit** on the land until his family moved to town, where they built a small cabin.

Life back then was different than it is now. When Harry was a boy in the 1950s, not many people used snowmobiles. Harry remembers riding on his father's dogsled, especially in the spring. He helped keep the dogs calm while his father hunted seal. He has lots of great memories of adventures they went on together. Harry learned a lot about how to be a musher from his dad.

*igluit (IG-lu-it): snow houses

Training puppies is one of Harry's earliest memories of dogsledding. He recalls that it was really important to be careful with the older dogs. Harry says you should not approach dogs you don't know.

That was okay, because he got to train puppies instead. He feels lucky to have worked with the puppies. It was a big responsibility, but it was also a lot of fun. Training puppies kept him busy!

When the puppies were a bit bigger, Harry and his friends leashed one or two puppies at a time to a little wooden sled. This way, young mushers like Harry could teach the puppies to pull. Many kids in Quaqtaq helped train the village's dogs. It's a lot of work to teach young puppies to be obedient. A champion musher must have highly trained dogs.

Harry liked to help out, but spending time with the puppies wasn't just about lending a hand. From a very young age, Harry dreamed of having his own dog team!

Growing Up

Harry went to school in Quaqtaq until Grade 6. Then he was sent far away from his home in Nunavik. He went to Churchill in northern Manitoba, which is all the way across Hudson Bay. He had to live at a type of school called a residential school. Life was very difficult at the school.
He wanted to leave and return home to Quaqtaq, where his family, community, and way of life were.

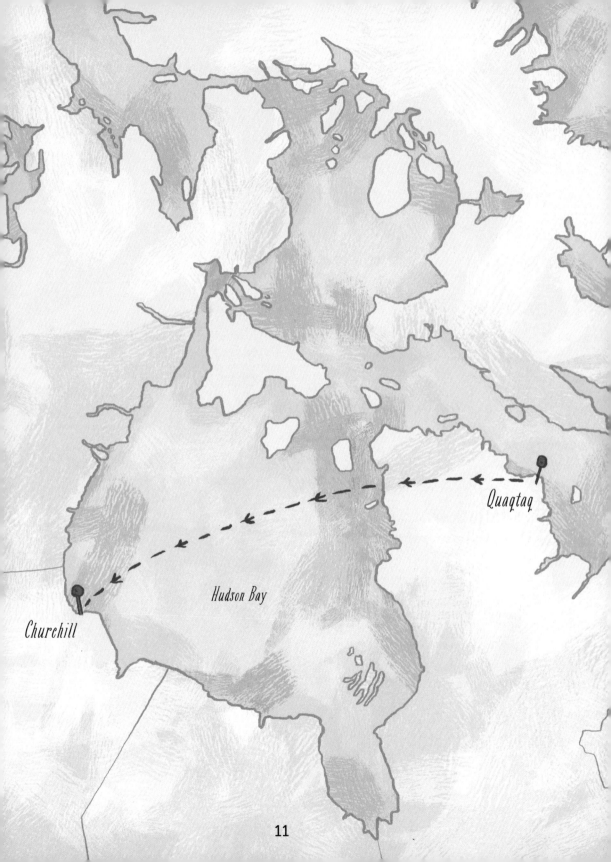

Quaqtaq

Hudson Bay

Churchill

After two years, Harry's wish came true.
He didn't have to go back to the school.
Instead, he stayed in his community
in Nunavik. It was time to learn to take
over his father's dog team.

But when Harry was still a boy, all of the
sled dogs in his region were killed. This
was a very difficult time for him, his family,
and the whole community. Losing the dogs
made travel on the land difficult and cut
the community off from one of their most
important traditions. Harry remembers
feeling like his hopes had been dashed.

Eventually, an Elder in the community brought in puppies from other places to build up a team again. As the dogs grew up and had puppies of their own, young mushers like Harry were able to form teams, too. It took years for the community to have as many dogs as it used to have.

Harry also had new challenges in training his team, because these dogs were not the same as the dogs his father had once had. They were different to train and had different personalities.

The Accident

On March 5, 1975, five days before his 22nd birthday, Harry and a few friends went seal hunting. They drove by snowmobile far out in Ungava Bay. It was a beautiful day and they were very successful in their hunt. Harry got three seals himself!

When it started to get dark, Harry and his friends loaded up the meat and gear on their *qamutiik.** Harry packed his gun but forgot to make sure the chamber was clear of bullets. As he pulled the rope to tighten his load, the gun went off and hit his leg. The bullet shattered his thigh bone.

*qamutiik (qa-mu-TEEK): sled

Harry's friends worked quickly to get him back to the community. Harry remembers being very cold on that snowmobile ride home.

When they got home, the nurse at the health centre realized Harry needed more medical help than they could give him in Quaqtaq. Harry was sent to a big hospital in Montreal. This was a very long way for him to go. Quaqtaq is as far north as you can go in Quebec, and Montreal is very far south from it. As you can imagine, Harry felt sad and alone in the hospital. He missed his community and being out on the land.

Quaqtaq

Montreal

19

Because Harry's injury was so bad, he was in the hospital for over two years. His injury wouldn't heal. In the end, Harry decided to allow doctors to amputate his leg, which means removing the leg in surgery. Harry was frightened, but he knew it was better to be healthy with one leg than to be sick and in pain with two legs.

The doctors who treated Harry said that even though the injury was serious, he had been lucky. If the bullet had hit him a little to the left or right, he might have died.

Life after the Accident

After he lost his leg, Harry wondered if he was going to be able to get a job or have a family. He wondered what kind of life he could have, or if he would be able to travel on the land again. Travelling on the land can be challenging even for a person with no disabilities. Harry was missing a leg and now used crutches. Would he lose his freedom and independence? The future was unknown for Harry.

Harry felt sorry for himself at first. He'd been through many difficulties. But when he started to learn how to adjust to life without his leg, he began to feel better. Harry had great friends and family who helped him.

It took five years for Harry to recover and learn how to be on the land with crutches. Now Harry uses crutches all the time. He takes them on his boat, on his snowmobile, and of course, with his dog team!

Good Friends

Even though Harry had learned how to move around on the land again, he didn't think he could be a musher anymore. His friends encouraged him to continue dogsledding. One friend challenged him, "Don't think you can't do it when you haven't tried. Try it first, then tell me you can't."

Harry slowly started to practise by going sledding with his friends. When he was ready, he got his own team.

When he looks back today, he knows he would never have tried to go dogsledding again if it weren't for his friends.

Adjustments

In Nunavik, mushers sit on their qamutiik
as their dogs run. From time to time, mushers
will stand up or run beside their qamutiik.

Harry has made adjustments to the way
he used to be a musher. He remains seated
all the time. If he is racing with a partner,
the partner will sometimes hop off and run
beside the qamutiik.

Harry builds his qamutiik slightly wider than others do. This way, there is room for his crutches. He also makes sure there is additional padding so that he is comfortable.

He has trained his dogs well to respond to his voice commands. The dogs are also used to Harry's crutches and the way he does things. For example, Harry sits on the ground when he puts harnesses on his dogs.

Raising a Team

After practising for a few years, Harry built up his dog team. It was hard work, but he trained all of his dogs himself. It is important for a musher to train his or her own dogs so that the musher and the dogs listen to each other and respect each other.

Having the dogs has helped him in so many ways. His most peaceful moments are when he is with his dogs. By persevering and believing in himself, he became a musher again. He let others encourage him, and now he encourages others to follow their dreams, too.

Harry's kids have all helped with the dogs over the years. Harry enjoys working together as a family and teaching his children how to train sled dogs. He feels that it is important for kids to get to know the land and develop the skills to travel safely.

In the fall, his family helps him get food for the winter ahead. Harry is fortunate to have a large boat to help him with hunting and fishing, too.

Current Team

Over the years, Harry has had dog teams of different sizes. Today, he has 12 dogs. When he runs his team to go hunting or exploring, he usually takes eight of the dogs with him. He makes sure all the dogs get a turn!

Harry doesn't just use his dog team for hunting. He is also a dogsled racer! When he is racing, he usually uses a team of 10 dogs.

Naming

Each dog is given a special name based on a physical characteristic or quality the dog has. They respond to their name when he calls them.

These are the names of his dogs:

Leaders
Taksaq
Siutik

Workers
Boy
Qiniq
Amauruq One
Amauraq Dear
Brownie
Taqsalaq
Qujuk
Siurautik
Sinangnaq
Takulik

Racing

Harry has been racing his team since 2002. Every year, he participates in the Ivakkak race in Nunavik. This is a very difficult race with many challenges for the participants, including trees, steep hills, and sharp turns. It takes about eight days to complete and can be dangerous! Teams travel about seven or eight hours a day.

By competing in the Ivakkak race, Harry has been able to heal from some of the hardships of his youth. The race has helped him to accept the loss of his community's dogs when he was a boy, as well as the loss of his leg. Dogs have always been part of traditional Inuit society. Racing a team of his own gives him the opportunity to connect with his culture.

Preparing for the Race

There is a lot to do to get ready for a race! Harry needs to make sure he isn't carrying too much on his qamutiik, because it has to be light.

Here is some of the equipment Harry has to take to be safe on the land when he races:

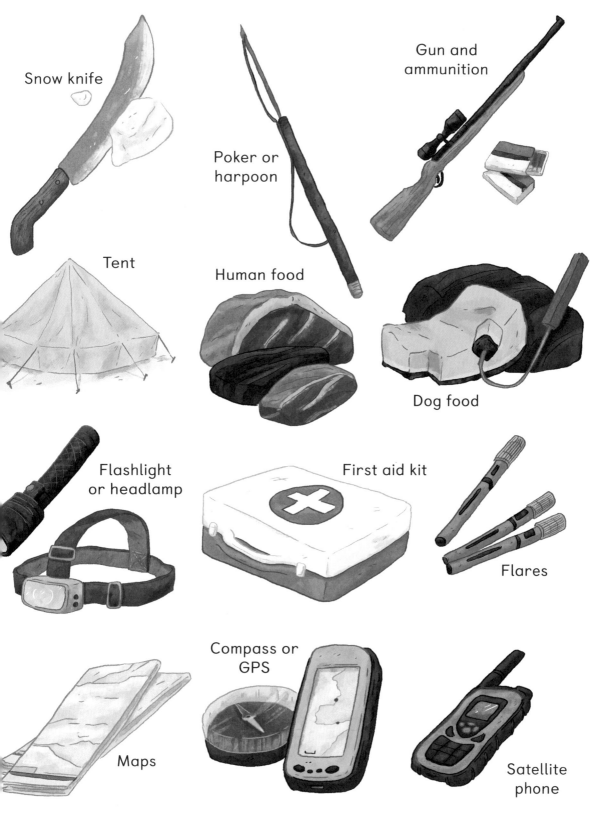

Snow knife

Poker or harpoon

Gun and ammunition

Tent

Human food

Dog food

Flashlight or headlamp

First aid kit

Flares

Maps

Compass or GPS

Satellite phone

45

Race Partners and Crew

For safety reasons, it is better to race with a partner instead of going alone. Harry has worked with many different partners over the years, including one of his sons.

The race partner rides on the qamutiik with the musher. Every dog team in the Ivakkak race must also have a support crew who drive snowmobiles along the route. The support crew help with the dogs, transport supplies, and set up camp.

47

Harry's Goals

There are usually about 15 teams in each race. Each night, all the racers and their partners and support crew camp together. Often, teams end the day by sharing fresh meat or fish and talking about stories from the trail. The racers are timed each day, and their totals are added up at the end of the race. The team with the fastest overall time wins.

Harry loves to compete and try his best. In his first few races, he came in last. Over the years, with hard work and practice, he has improved his times. His personal best is third place!

Harry's goal is to help young people learn how to raise and lead a team. He is now competing against a former student and race partner. That brings him a lot of satisfaction. He has also given the puppies of many of his dogs to other racers.

Living with a disability has taught Harry a lot about himself, and he feels much stronger as a result. Dogsledding has been an extremely important part of his life. It has helped him heal from the difficult things he has faced in his life. Dogsledding has also helped him connect with Inuit tradition.

Tips for Future Dog Team Owners

Harry wants to inspire young people to participate in dogsledding. Here are his tips for young mushers:

1. Always feed your dogs and take care of them. If dogs are hungry, they won't be strong and fast.

2. Respect your dogs. Give them positive attention, and never hurt them.

3. Make sure your dogs have lots of water to drink in summer and clean snow to eat in winter.

4. Pet your dogs every day so they know you. Get puppies familiar with voice commands.

5. Always obey the regulations in your community as a dog owner. Be respectful of other community members.

Nunavummi
Reading Series

The Nunavummi reading series is a Nunavut-developed levelled book series that supports literacy development while teaching readers about the people, traditions, and environment of the Canadian Arctic.

- 24–40 pages
- Sentences are complex and vary in length
- Lots of varied punctuation
- Dialogue is included in fiction texts and is necessary to understand the story
- Readers rely on the words to decode the text; images are present but only somewhat supportive

- 24–56 pages
- Sentences can be more complicated and are not always restricted to a structure that readers are familiar with
- Some unfamiliar themes and genres are introduced
- Readers rely on the words to decode the text; images are present but only somewhat supportive

- 24–64 pages
- Chapter books introduced
- Readers may be exposed to new genres (science fiction, mysteries, biographies, etc.) and unfamiliar themes and settings
- Illustrations are somewhat supportive and may not be included on every spread of pages

Fountas & Pinnell Text Level: N

This book has been officially levelled using the F&P Text Level Gradient™ Leveling System.